CW01631647

£4.99
3/41

to Pod
love Ros
x

THE FOOLS OF CHELM
and Their History

THIS IS THE NATURAL PORTRAIT OF THE FAMOUS CITY OF:
CHELM: חלם
RIVER
LET THERE BE CHELM!
ROAD
TREE
ROAD
CHELM
ALL ROADS LEAD TO: CHELM
CHELM
ROAD
HEAD
ROAD
TOE
ROAD
BOOKS
CHELM
RIVER
ROAD
N
E
W
S
EARLY CHELMITES
LATER CHELMITES
MODERN CHELMITES
BRAINS
NOSE
EAR

THE FOOLS OF CHELM
and Their History

Isaac Bashevis Singer
translated by the Author and Elizabeth Shub
Illustrated by Uri Shulevitz

Abelard · London

First published in the United States of America
in 1973 by Farrar, Straus and Giroux, New York.
First published in Great Britain in 1975
by Abelard-Schuman Limited.

ISBN 0 200 72276 X

Abelard-Schuman Limited
450 Edgware Road
London W2
and
Kingswood House
Heath and Reach
Leighton Buzzard
Bedfordshire

Printed in Great Britain by
Compton Printing Ltd., Aylesbury

THE FOOLS OF CHELM
and Their History

How Chelm Came to Be

There was no agreement among the scholars of Chelm on how the town came into existence. The pious believed that God said, ''Let there be Chelm.'' And there was Chelm. But many scholars insisted that the town happened as the result of an eruption.

''Before Chelm,'' they said, ''the area was one huge chaos, all fog and mist. Then came a great explosion and Chelm appeared.''

At the beginning the surface of Chelm was so hot that even if Chelmites had already existed, they could not have walked on the earth because they would have burned their feet. But slowly Chelm cooled and was covered by a crust, like a pot of porridge that has been left standing. The first Chelmites, the scholars say, were not people but microbes, amoebas, and other such creatures. Later a river formed in Chelm. It contained many fish, and these were the ancestors of the Chelmites. This may be the reason why the Chelmites love fish, especially gefilte fish.

The first Chelmites could neither read nor write, and the history of those ancient times was never recorded. It is said that these earliest Chelmites were primitive people. They walked around naked and barefoot, lived in caves, and hunted animals with axes and spears made of stone. They often starved and were sick. But since the word "crisis" did not exist yet, there were no crises and no one tried to solve them.

After many, many years the Chelmites became civilized. They learned to read and write, and such words as "problem" and "crisis" were created. The moment the word "crisis" appeared in the language, the people realized there was a crisis in Chelm. They saw that things were not good in their town. The inventor of these words was a man called Gronam. Or, as he is known, Gronam the First. He was also called Gronam Ox because he sported a headdress with the horns of an ox.

Gronam was the first sage of Chelm, as well as its first ruler. In Chelm, rulership and wisdom have always gone together. A council of five sages helped Gronam govern. They were: Dopey Lekisch, Zeinvel Ninny, Treitel Fool, Sender Donkey, and Shmendrick Numskull. Gronam also had a secretary, who was called Shlemiel.

One day Gronam ordered Shlemiel to summon the sages to a council.

When they assembled, Gronam said, "My sages, there is a crisis in Chelm. Most of our citizens haven't enough bread to eat, they are dressed in rags, and many of them are suffering from coughs and sniffles. How can we solve this crisis?"

The sages thought for seven days and seven nights, as was their custom.

Then Gronam said, "The time is up. Let me hear what you have to say."

Dopey Lekisch was the first to speak. "There are only a few

people in Chelm educated enough to know that 'crisis' means a bad situation. Let's make a law forbidding the word's use, and it will soon be forgotten. Then no one will know that there is a crisis, and we the sages will not have to rack our brains to solve it."

"Too late," Zeinvel Ninny interrupted. "It is true that the old people don't know the word, but the younger generation have all learned it, and they represent the future of Chelm."

"What do you suggest, Zeinvel Ninny?" asked Gronam Ox.

"My advice," Zeinvel Ninny said, "is that there should be two fast days each week, namely Monday and Thursday. In this way we will save a lot of bread and there will no longer be a bread shortage."

"That would solve the bread problem, but what about the scarcity of clothing and shoes?" Gronam Ox asked.

Treitel Fool placed two fingers on his nose as a signal that he had something to say.

"Speak, Treitel Fool," Gronam ordered.

"My advice," said Treitel Fool, "is that we put high taxes on shoes, boots, caftans, pants, vests, skirts, petticoats, and all other articles of clothing. The poor will not be able to afford

any clothes. This will leave more than enough for the rich. Why worry about the poor?"

"Bad advice!" exclaimed Sender Donkey.

"Why is this bad advice?" asked Gronam Ox.

"It is bad because the poor are the ones who work in the fields and shops. If they are ragged and unshod, they will always suffer from colds, coughs, and sniffles and thus be unable to work. They will not be able to produce enough bread and clothes even for the rich."

"And what do you suggest, Sender Donkey?"

"I suggest," Sender Donkey replied, "that at night, when the rich are asleep, the poor should break into their houses and take their boots, slippers, caftans, dresses, and whatever else they possess. The poor will then be properly dressed and they will be able to work in the fields and shops without catching cold. Why worry about the rich?"

"All wrong," announced Shmendrick Numskull.

"Why is it all wrong?" Gronam asked.

"Because for each rich man in Chelm there are some hundred paupers," said Shmendrick Numskull. "There will not be enough clothes to go around. Besides, the rich are all potbellied and the poor are skinny, so the rich people's clothes won't fit.''

''What is your solution, Shmendrick Numskull?'' asked Gronam Ox.

''I say that clothes should be abolished altogether. The great historians of Chelm tell us that in ancient times our ancestors went about naked and dwelt in caves. They lived by hunting. Let's do the same, and all our problems will be solved.''

''That's nonsense,'' said Dopey Lekisch. ''According to our scholars, in ancient times there were no winters in Chelm. That's why the people walked about naked. Now I suggest that we postpone our meeting. It seems that seven days and seven nights of pondering have not been enough.''

For a moment it looked as if Gronam Ox was about to accept this clever suggestion. It was the usual thing, when the sages of Chelm could not come to a satisfactory decision, to postpone the discussion until a future meeting. Gronam had already lifted his gavel to knock three times as an indication that the meeting was adjourned, when he suddenly clutched his bulging forehead and said, ''My highly esteemed sages, I have a solution.''

''What is your solution, Sage of Sages?'' the others asked.

''Be still and listen.''

Each sage pulled the lobe of his left ear, and intoned, ''Yes, Gronam Ox, we are all ears.''

Who Is the Enemy?

"My idea," said Gronam Ox, "is that only a war can save Chelm."

"A war?" all five sages called out in astonishment.

Until that time, Chelm had never waged war. It had a small police force and the policemen carried sticks, but there were no soldiers in Chelm.

"Yes, a war," Gronam Ox repeated.

"A war with whom?" asked Dopey Lekisch.

"A war with the people of Gorshkov."

"What have the people of Gorshkov done that we should make war on them?" asked Zeinvel Ninny.

"How can we make war if we have neither swords nor spears?" asked Treitel Fool.

"How can a war with Gorshkov help us?" asked Sender Donkey. "Gorshkov is a tiny village and the people there are even poorer than we are."

"And what guarantee is there that we will win?" put in Shmendrick Numskull. "And who will do the fighting?"

"These are good questions," Gronam Ox declared. "Here is my answer:

"We will make war on the people of Gorshkov because they call us fools. We Chelmites know that, of the ten measures of wisdom sent down to earth from heaven, nine went to Chelm. But the conceited people of Gorshkov think they are the clever ones and we the fools. The only way to convince them that we are cleverer than they is to beat them at war. It is true that we have neither swords nor spears. But we have Zalman Blacksmith and he can make them for us. It is true that we must buy our iron in Lublin and it is very expensive, but our women have iron pots and pans, and since there isn't much to cook in any case, they can just as well let their pots be turned into swords and spears. It is also true that Gorshkov is small and the people are poorer than we are, but when we are victorious we will make slaves of our enemies and they will do our work for us. And we will be able to devote all our time to clever thoughts, as befits the wise men of Chelm. As for the outcome of the war, there is no need to worry: for every Gorshkov fool, there are ten wise men of Chelm. We have many young men who go around idle; we will recruit them for the army. To be absolutely sure of victory, we will attack Gorshkov in the dead of night, and before they wake up to what has happened, they will have been killed or captured and made slaves."

"Gronam Ox, you are not only the greatest sage of Chelm but of the whole world," Dopey Lekisch proclaimed.

"When we conquer Gorshkov, Chelm will become an empire," added Zeinvel Ninny.

"Gronam Ox will be King of Chelm and Emperor of Gorshkov," said Treitel Fool.

"The first thing we will order our slaves to do is build the King and Emperor a castle consisting of three rooms and a kitchen,'' said Sender Donkey. ''One of them will be your thinking room; there your wife, Yente Pesha, the Empress, will not be able to disturb your meditations with her nagging and scolding.''

Shlemiel opened his mouth wide and stuck out his tongue, which meant that he wanted to speak.

''What do you have to say?'' Gronam asked. ''You forget that you are only a secretary and not one of my councillors.''

''Please forgive me, Super Sage, future King and Emperor. What I want to say will benefit Chelm and contribute to the successful outcome of the war as well.''

''What is it? Be brief.''

''Gorshkov is quite a distance from here—about eight miles. There is no road from Chelm to Gorshkov, and one has to cross a forest and a swamp to get there. How will our heroic soldiers find their way, especially as the battle is to take place in the middle of the night? Besides, Gorshkov has a wall around it and the gate is locked at sundown. How will our heroes invade Gorshkov if the gate is locked?''

There was silence. No one had expected Shlemiel to ask such a difficult question.

Dopey Lekisch was the first to speak. "This malicious question is a betrayal of the Empire!" he shouted angrily.

"He should be imprisoned and sentenced to hard labour," said Zeinvel Ninny.

"And never be set free, until the end of the world," added Treitel Fool.

"He should be hanged!" exclaimed Sender Donkey.

"To hang him once is not enough!" shouted Shmendrick Numskull. "He should be hanged at least three times."

"My devoted councillors," Gronam said, "it is not necessary to be so hard on Shlemiel. Let's not forget he is the only Shlemiel we have, and if he is hanged even once, we will be left without a Shlemiel. In any case, I have an answer to his question."

"So quickly?" all five councillors asked as if with one voice.

"My brain wastes no time," Gronam replied. "There is a man called Haskel who happens to have been born in Gorshkov but who is married to a woman from Chelm. He certainly knows the way to Gorshkov and he will lead us. As for the gate, Feitel Thief is in jail serving a sentence of three hundred years for breaking into Berel's grocery store and stealing three

onions. Since he was able to break open the lock of Berel's grocery store, he will surely be able to unlock the one on the Gorshkov gate. I, Gronam, will set him free and he will get our brave troops into Gorshkov without any trouble."

The councillors were so impressed with Gronam's wisdom that they were speechless.

Shlemiel again opened his mouth wide and stuck out his tongue, but before he could utter a word, Gronam Ox said, "Better close your mouth or you'll find yourself a head shorter. The meeting is adjourned. It is my imperial command that all that has been discussed at this council remain a state secret. You are dismissed."

The news spread immediately throughout Chelm that Gronam Ox was preparing to wage war against Gorshkov and that the plan was a highly guarded secret.

The War

In Chelm it was always easier to talk than to act. Zalman Blacksmith was not very skilled at forging swords and spears. When Yente Pesha, Gronam's wife, heard that she would have to sacrifice her pots and pans for military purposes, she poured her vilest curses on Gronam. ''We have enough trouble without a war,'' she screamed at him. ''You not only wear the horns of an ox but you have the brains of one.''

''Yente Pesha, don't forget that you're addressing the future Emperor of Gorshkov,'' Gronam admonished her.

''Emperor, shmemperor,'' Yente Pesha replied. ''To me you're nothing but a fool of Chelm.''

Anyone else who had spoken in such a way to Gronam would immediately have been tried as a traitor. But against Yente Pesha and her big mouth, even Gronam was helpless.

Spring came and the young men of Chelm, instead of working in the fields, were mustered into the army and put in training for the Gorshkov war. As a result, there was a meagre harvest.

Autumn arrived and the rains began. Since the soldiers either went barefoot or had torn boots, many caught cold. Almost the whole army was coughing and sniffling. But it was impossible to postpone the war. One dark night, under the leadership of Gronam Ox himself, the army of Chelm marched toward Gorshkov. In the front ranks were Haskel, the pathfinder, and Feitel Thief. It had been raining for three whole days and the soldiers sank to their knees in the mud. To keep up the army's morale Zeckel, the court poet, composed a song.

Heroes of Chelm are we,
Marching to set Gorshkov free.
Led by Gronam the Wise,
We'll take the fools by surprise.
Heroes of Chelm rejoice,
Gronam Ox is our choice.

Most of the soldiers were hoarse. Many had cut their feet on stones as they waded through the mud. But everybody knows that war is not child's play.

Hours passed and there was no sign of Gorshkov.

Gronam became impatient. "Haskel, where is Gorshkov?" he asked.

"I'm afraid I've made a mistake," Haskel said timidly, after some hesitation. "Instead of turning right, I turned left, and we are approaching Mazelborsht."

"Mazelborsht!" the officers cried out in rage.

"I'm afraid so," said Haskel. "But what's the difference? Mazelborsht has even fewer soldiers than Gorshkov and it will be easier to conquer."

Shlemiel, who had accompanied the army, said, "We've

come to fight the people of Gorshkov because they think we're fools, but what do we have against the people of Mazelborsht?"

As always, Gronam found an answer immediately. "The people of Mazelborsht also think we're fools. The truth is, the whole world considers us fools. No matter whom we attack, it will be exactly what they deserve."

"Hurrah! Long live Gronam, our Emperor!" the troops cheered.

"Long live Chelm! Death to the Mazelborshters!"

Most of the citizens of Mazelborsht were peacefully asleep that night. No one even dreamed about war. There was no wall or gate in Mazelborsht and Feitel Thief did not have to break open the gate lock. The truth is, there were no locks at all in Mazelborsht. The Chelmites could have had an easy victory. But it so happened that on that very night, the wedding of a butcher boy from Gorshkov and the daughter of a Mazelborsht coachman was taking place. As was the custom, the wedding was being held in the bride's village. The guests—the butchers and the coachmen—were still drinking and dancing when suddenly they heard voices singing, cheering. They went out and saw a mob approaching, some armed with swords and spears, others with sticks. One Chelmite, for lack of something better, carried a long wooden pestle used for grinding matzo flour.

When the wedding guests asked what this was all about, Gronam Ox said, "We are the army of Chelm. We planned to attack Gorshkov because the people there call us fools, but our guide Haskel took a wrong turn and brought us to Mazelborsht. And since you people of Mazelborsht also call us fools, we have decided to make war on you."

That's all the butchers and coachmen needed to hear. They were drunk and threw themselves on the army of Chelm with wild fury. Gronam and his officers called on the soldiers of Chelm to fight back.

"The honour of Chelm is in your hands, heroic soldiers!" Gronam shouted desperately. "Show the whole world that Chelmites are not only shrewd but mighty warriors too."

But Gronam's words were of little help to the army of Chelm. The soldiers were worn out from marching and from lack of sleep and they were wet from the rain. They ran. The drummers dropped their drums. Some of those who carried swords tried to get them out of their scabbards, but their

hands were numb with cold. In a few minutes the army of Chelm suffered a complete rout.

Around the butcher shops of Mazelborsht there were many stray dogs and they ran after the retreating army, barking and biting. One of the dogs tore the pants off a fleeing soldier.

The rest of the people of Mazelborsht went on sleeping, unaware that they had slept through a historic victory.

The following day, toward dusk, the army of Chelm returned home half naked, barefoot, weaponless, with broken noses and black eyes. The women and girls of Chelm had prepared a warm welcome for the victors. They had cooked blintzes and made sour cream and set out pitchers of berry juice. Now they wept bitterly. Thank God, no one had been killed, but a few soldiers and one general were missing. They had either been captured or had decided to remain with the enemy in Mazelborsht.

Gronam Ox had lost one of his horns. His left eye was swollen from a blow from a butcher boy. Yente Pesha was just stepping out of the house to empty the slops when she caught sight of him. She was so startled that she poured the bucketful over Gronam's feet.

"Woe is me! They've put better than you in the grave!" she wailed.

Gronam Ox and his sages took counsel. They pondered seven days and seven nights, at the end of which they issued the following proclamation:

1. Gronam Ox remains the Sage of Sages, ruler of Chelm, and victorious Emperor of Mazelborsht.

2. In the future, before an attack on the enemy, spies are to be sent out to make sure that butchers and coachmen are not attending a wedding that evening.

3. Pestles for grinding matzo flour are never again to be used as weapons by the Chelm army.

4. When the army of Chelm returns from battle, Yente Pesha, the Empress, is not to greet the Emperor by pouring slops over his feet.

These orders were inscribed on parchment and signed by Gronam and his five sages.

Gronam Ox voiced the feelings of all Chelmites when he said, "This war has not made us rich, but it has made us wise."

The Revolt

It is known that a lost war sooner or later is followed by a revolt. And that is what happened in Chelm.

The leader of the Revolutionary Party, Bunem Pokraka proclaimed: "Gronam Ox has misled us. Chelm is disgraced. We are the laughingstock of Gorshkov, Mazelborsht, Izbitza, and even Lublin."

Bunem Pokraka set forth the following revolutionary programme:

1. Gronam Ox is to abdicate. He must be forced to do so of his own free will.

2. Money is abolished. As long as money exists, there are rich and there are poor. Without money, everyone will be equally poor. There will be no thieves, and the city will not have to pay salaries to Chaikel the policeman and Lemel the jailer.

3. Chelm is to be ruled not by one Sage of Sages but by three, under the leadership of Bunem Pokraka, the Supreme Sage of Sages.

4. Elections will be held every forty years, on Purim. Only members of the Revolutionary Party will be eligible to vote.

5. The women of Chelm will donate their gold jewellery to be melted down and used for a statue of Bunem Pokraka.

6. Zeckel Poet is to compose a hymn in praise of Bunem Pokraka. It must be 12,000 lines long, and all schoolchildren will learn it by heart.

7. Shlemiel, because he was opposed to the war, is appointed secretary to Bunem Pokraka.

8. Gronam and his five sages are sentenced to imprisonment forever and a Wednesday.

9. Yente Pesha, because she poured slops over Gronam's feet, need not accompany her husband to jail. Instead, she is to divorce Gronam and marry Shlemiel.

This revolutionary program was enthusiastically received by the poor of Chelm. Many of those who in the past had admired Gronam's wisdom now called him an idiot, an ass, and a ne'er-do-well. Zeckel Poet, who had written countless poems in praise of Gronam, now sat down to write an ode to Bunem Pokraka. He complained that 12,000 lines were not enough to describe all of Bunem Pokraka's virtues. The ode began:

It shall be known for now and ever
Bunem Pokraka is mighty and clever.

Bunem Pokraka announced that he would take over the government the day before the Feast of Shevuoth. As a rule, this time of year is sunny and mild and the Chelmites look forward to the blintzes they will eat on the holiday. By chance, it also happened to be Bunem Pokraka's birthday.

When Gronam and his sages learned what was about to happen, they were seized with fear. To be imprisoned forever and a Wednesday is no small matter. Gronam immediately called a meeting of his council. As always, the meeting took place in his house. But this time Yente Pesha cornered the sages before they could begin.

"Gronam Ox," she shouted, "you deserve what has befallen you. You are as much a sage as I am a chimney sweep. The whole world is in stitches over your war with Mazelborsht. Nevertheless, I have no intention of divorcing you. And I will not marry Shlemiel. There is no sense in exchanging one shlemiel for another."

Shlemiel, who was there to take the minutes of the meeting, opened his mouth and stuck out his tongue, indicating his desire to speak. But Gronam spoke first. "Have no fear, Shlemiel," he said. "No one will drag you to the wedding canopy."

As usual, the meeting lasted a long time, and as usual, Gronam listened to the advice of all five sages. Dopey Lekisch suggested that Gronam and the sages shave their beards and shorten their caftans so they would not be recognized, and thus escape imprisonment. Zeinvel Ninny thought it might not be too late to bribe Bunem Pokraka by offering him Shlemiel's job. Treitel Fool proposed that, since they still had a few broken swords and spears, they might use them to drive off the rebels, even though the whole town and the army were on the rebels' side. Sender Donkey pointed out a loophole in Bunem Pokraka's programme. Since the rebels were going to do away with money—and with the jailer too, because there would be nothing to pay him with—how would they be able to keep the sages in prison forever and a Wednesday? Shmendrick Numskull concluded that it would be best to plead with Bunem Pokraka to shorten their sentence at least by the Wednesday.

Gronam nodded, shook his head, and said solemnly, "My beloved sages, I have heard your wise words and, as always, admired them immensely. Just the same, I am unable to accept your advice."

"What do you suggest?" the sages chorused.

"I suggest that we flee from Chelm."

"Flee from Chelm!" the sages chorused again, this time in consternation.

"I understand how you feel," Gronam said. "Although Chelm has been the wisest town in the world, if the Chelmites are prepared to replace us with Bunem Pokraka and his henchmen, that can only mean that Chelm is no longer itself."

"What will happen to our wives and children?"

"They will wait for us until Chelm comes to its senses and we can return."

"How will we live in exile?"

"We will take the treasury money with us. The rebels of Chelm don't believe in money, but in Lublin money is still money. Who knows, perhaps it is destined that we carry the wisdom of Chelm to other cities."

"We've never heard you speak more brilliantly," said Dopey Lekisch.

"I will go with you," Shlemiel announced, not even bothering to ask for permission to speak.

"Why should you run away?" Gronam asked. "You are in favour with the revolutionaries. They even want to give you my Yente Pesha as a wife."

"That's why I want to run away," Shlemiel said. "I don't want to be nagged by her the way you are."

"Very well, you may come with us."

That night Gronam, the five sages, and Shlemiel left Chelm, taking with them the chest containing Chelm's treasury. But when they opened it, they found it empty. Feitel Thief, who had been released from prison, had crept into the vault and taken everything.

Gronam Ox was disappointed. "When I return to Chelm as ruler," he announced, "and go to war with Gorshkov, I will certainly not free Feitel Thief to break open the lock of the Gorshkov gate."

"Then who will break open the lock?" Shmendrick Numskull asked.

"We will attack during the day, when the gate is open," Gronam replied.

Chelm without Money

When it was discovered that Gronam and his five sages had run off with the town treasury, Chelm rang with shouts of "Long live Bunem Pokraka! Long live the revolution!" Bunem was in full power.

Soon, however, trouble began.

Bunem Pokraka had abolished money, but the merchants refused to part with their goods for nothing. Bunem Pokraka's men confiscated the stores and put government managers in charge. But the managers distributed the goods among their friends, and new merchandise could not be obtained. Soon, on all sides, the cry went up: "Give us back money! We want money!"

Bunem Pokraka tried to explain that gold cannot be eaten, and neither can bank notes. "Then what shall we buy food with?" the Chelmites asked.

Bunem Pokraka and his two Sages of Sages, Berel Pinhead and Shmerel Thickwit, pondered for three days and three nights and then they decreed that three times a week, on Monday, Tuesday, and Thursday, all Chelmites would gather at the marketplace to barter their goods. The proclamation was issued on Wednesday, and on Thursday many Chelmites came to the marketplace.

The first to appear was Zeckel Poet. He set up a stand, spread his poems on the counter, and called out, "I will exchange my poems for bread, butter, cheese, chickens, eggs, onions, garlic. The sole of my left boot is worn through; I offer a poem of twenty-three lines to the shoemaker who will fix it. Fleckel the critic has written that there never was a poet like Zeckel Poet and there never will be!"

Shmoyger the matchmaker did not bring his merchandise with him—that is, the boys and girls—but he was heard chanting, "My wife, Keila Basha, can't prepare the Sabbath meal because our larder is empty. For making a match I will take a sack of rye flour for dark bread, a sack of white flour for the Sabbath loaves, ten pounds of groats, ten pounds of rice, and one pound of chicken fat for the Sabbath pudding. Boys and girls, come to me and I will make you a match."

The Chelm band, three fiddlers and a drummer, stood together. The drummer was the barker. "If you want to hear music, gather around. For a chicken we'll play a polka; for a duck we'll play a mazurka; and for a side of beef, a whole concerto."

Fultsha Jester announced in singsong: "I sell jokes. If you want to burst with laughter, come to me. A joke for an egg. Three jokes for two eggs. Five jokes for three eggs."

But that day no one in Chelm was in need of poetry, matchmaking, music, or jokes. One shoemaker was prepared to barter a pair of boots for a goat, but the owner of the goat figured out that in the days when there had been money the goat would have been worth three boots. But what does one do with three

boots? The shoemaker and the goat owner haggled all day long and did not strike a bargain.

The following day, Friday, Hotzmach the bath attendant did not heat the bath because he hadn't received any wages. On Saturday, half of Chelm fasted. Sunday morning a huge crowd gathered in front of Bunem Pokraka's house and wild screams were heard.

"Give us money. Chelm cannot exist without money. We want money!"

That night Bunem Pokraka, Berel Pinhead, and Shmerel Thickwit did not sleep a wink. Stones were thrown at the windows of Bunem's house. His wife, who was as much a shrew as Gronam's Yente Pesha, screamed vile curses at her husband.

Suddenly a voice was heard in the crowd outside.

"Brothers and sisters of Chelm, Bunem Pokraka has betrayed the revolution. He is an enemy of the people and even stupider than Gronam Ox. I, Feitel Thief, am taking over the government of Chelm. I will immediately issue new money. Long live the revolution! Down with Bunem Pokraka! I, Feitel, pronounce myself the First Sage of Chelm forever after."

"Down with Bunem Pokraka! Long live Feitel!" was heard from the crowd.

Feitel Thief and his two assistants, Notke Knife and Yoshke Pickpocket, led the crowd to a hideout and showed them the gold they had stolen from Gronam Ox's treasury. But instead of issuing gold coins to the people, they handed out paper money. Since neither Feitel nor his assistants could write, the bank notes had three circles printed on them. In one hour's time, order was restored in Chelm. Bunem Pokraka, Berel Pinhead, and Shmerel Thickwit were imprisoned and charged with treason. The verdict of the court could be predicted—imprisonment forever and a Wednesday.

That day Zeckel Poet began tailoring his ode to fit Feitel Thief. But the lines allowed for Bunem, he maintained, would not be nearly enough to describe Feitel's great accomplishments. Zeckel said he needed at least twice that number.

Feitel's Reign

Feitel's first official act after issuing paper money was to imprison the judge who had sentenced him for theft in Gronam's time. Then he dictated a new set of laws to his secretary:

1. Stealing is no longer a crime, except if one steals from a thief.

2. The citizens of Chelm are to pay three quarters of their income in taxes. In addition, every Thursday, the women of Chelm will present to the government two pieces of gefilte

fish, a plate of carrot stew, three slices of ḥallah, and a Sabbath pudding.

3. War is again declared on Gorshkov and Mazelborsht. Chelm will avenge itself for the defeat suffered at the hands of coachmen and butchers.

4. All knives, axes, meat cleavers, forks, as well as penknives and hairpins, are confiscated for the use of the army.

5. All men between the ages of eleven and eighty are to train half a day every day in preparation for the coming battle.

6. Chelm is again declared an empire that will eventually take in all the territory between the river San and the river Bug.

7. All foreigners, when meeting a native of Chelm, are to bow seven times, exclaiming, "Long live Feitel."

8. If a Chelmite hits a foreigner and knocks out one of his teeth, the foreigner is to pay his attacker the amount he would have had to pay a dentist to have the tooth extracted.

9. The old holidays are abolished. The anniversary of the day Feitel picked his first pocket is henceforth declared a national holiday! Additional holidays are the anniversaries of the days on which Feitel cracked his first lock and made his first holdup. There is to be no more Sabbath.

When the new laws were made public, the older people of Chelm were badly frightened and predicted that nothing good would come of them. But the toughs of Chelm sided with Feitel. Since there were no barracks in Chelm to house the new army, Feitel ordered that the paupers and the sick be driven out of the poorhouse and that it be taken over by the military.

Before long, Feitel's army began to win great victories. They marched on Gorshkov at night. The gate was broken open by Feitel himself, and the people of Gorshkov were forced to surrender. Mazelborsht suffered the same fate. The mighty army of Chelm conquered a few other hamlets as well on the journey home.

In his victory ode, Zeckel Poet foretold that the army of Chelm would one day conquer India, Izbitza, Ethiopia, Frampol, and Madagascar.

But it was not long before there was a crisis in Feitel's regime. All the able-bodied men had been recruited into the army, and there was no one left to do the work. Again there was a lack of food, clothing, and shoes. Feitel had brought in some slaves, former citizens of Gorshkov and Mazelborsht, but there was nothing to feed them with.

After Feitel declared that stealing was no longer a crime, there were so many thefts that honest people had no possessions left. The thieves then began to steal from one another, and there was a lot of fighting among Feitel's followers.

Soon the news came that the cities of Lublin, Zamosc, Krasnostav, Bilgoray, Frampol, and Izbitza were mobilizing to fight Chelm. Feitel in turn mobilized all of Chelm, even the sick, who had been driven out of the poorhouse. But the starving Chelmites could not withstand an army that was fresh, well fed, and properly armed. Chelm was besieged. Feitel insisted that Chelm would overcome its enemies and the new order would last forever. But a week after the siege started, the army of Chelm resembled an army of corpses.

When Feitel realized that the end had come, he hid in the community steam bath. However, he was soon found. His captors put a garbage can on his head, made him carry a broom in one hand and a paper sword in the other, and he was led into the market square in disgrace.

Zeckel Poet had already written 16,000 lines in praise of Feitel before the siege began. When he saw that things were

FEITEL!
F
CHELM

going badly, he made some changes in the poem and called it "The Shame and Downfall of Feitel Tyrant."

The Chelmites were afraid that their conquerors would enslave them and condemn them to hard labour in Gorshkov and Mazelborsht. But those towns were not in need of slaves. They had enough unemployed of their own.

When Gronam Ox and his five sages heard that Chelm had been liberated, they returned to Chelm, bringing the empty money chest with them. Yente Pesha was so surprised to see her husband that she poured out the slops, this time on his bare feet. Gronam and his five sages, who had been beggars in Lublin, became again the rulers of Chelm.

The Future Is Bright

Chelm no longer had military ambitions, and the Chelmites set to work enthusiastically. It was clear that only work could save them.

They became so industrious that they scarcely had time to eat. They produced more than they could sell and began to look for markets outside Chelm. But the people of Gorshkov and Mazelborsht, who might have bought many of Chelm's products, had no money. Gronam and his sages thought for seven days and seven nights and came up with a solution. They would give Mazelborsht and Gorshkov money so they could buy the goods produced by Chelm.

This decision was approved by the merchants of Chelm, but some of the poor objected. "Why give money to Gorshkov and Mazelborsht, our former enemies," they said, "while we veterans starve?" There were protests and demonstrations, and a new crisis arose in Chelm.

In exile in the city of Izbitza, Bunem Pokraka proclaimed that money was at the root of Chelm's misfortunes. He sent his agents to Chelm to spread the word among the people that Bunem Pokraka was the only one who could save Chelm.

When Gronam realized that his regime was tottering once more, he decided to create an additional council, consisting of a hundred Chelmite undersages. This council was to sit day and night all year round and solve all problems as they came up. Naturally, its decisions would have to be reviewed by Gronam and his five sages. Gronam appointed as president of the new council the most famous philosopher of Chelm, Vizusu, author of a ten-volume study on which came first, the chicken or the egg.

The Council of the Hundred Undersages, as it was called, sat for many years, but it never made a decision, as there was continuous disagreement and bickering among the Undersages. Blows, name-calling, and the throwing of inkwells were daily occurrences. Some of the Undersages dared to call Vizusu "Chelmite idiot."

Yente Pesha, who was an ardent observer of what went on in the council and the government, decided that the men of Chelm were such big fools that they could never solve the crises of the city. She founded a Women's Party. Its platform provided for the men of Chelm to take over the housework, the sweeping of floors, the washing of nappies, the cooking and baking, and the care of infants. Meanwhile, the women of Chelm would run the government. As a result of all this, there were many quarrels between Gronam and Yente Pesha, as well as between the other sages and their wives.

After supper Yente Pesha would say, "Gronam Ox, it's time for you to wash the dishes."

"I, Gronam, the Supersage, should wash dishes? And what will you do?"

"I will read Vizusu's new book, *What Would Have Happened*

CHELM YENTES UNITE!
MEN TO KITCHEN
WOMEN TO POWER

to the Chelmites if Chelm Never Existed," Yente Pesha would reply.

"This is the end of the world," Gronam would protest.

"Not the end of the world but the end of your tyranny," Yente Pesha would say. "Don't lose time, Gronam. Take off your crown, put on the apron, and get busy."

And even though Gronam considered washing dishes a degradation for a super-ruler, he did exactly as Yente Pesha told him, because for men to wash dishes had become the fashion in Chelm, and it is known that in Chelm the fashion is even stronger than the law.

This is more or less the history of Chelm up to the present time. But Gronam remains optimistic. In his most recent speech, made at the unveiling of the newest monument in his honour, he said:

"We do not wish to conquer the world, but our wisdom is spreading throughout it just the same. The future is bright. The chances are good that someday the whole world will be one great Chelm."